Congratulations!

For what you may ask? Congratulations for making a decision to bet on yourself today. Congratulations for taking a step toward achieving your dreams and fulfilling your screenwriting goals. Congratulations for setting the proverbial dinner table for all of the great things that are to come for you. And congratulations for having the clarity to understand not a single thing will happen until you write that script! Our expectations are high, as yours no doubt are, too. We are devoted to helping you achieve a story to set you apart from all the other writers. We are delighted to help you on your journey.

You are unique, and we think that is important. Utilize the skills, knowledge and experiences that set you apart and can shape your stories.

Screenwriting isn't "easy," or everyone would do it. As you progress through this challenge, you will be exposed to many new terms, and processes. It will be like learning a new language because, well, you are! I highly recommend saving things in a file that you can easily access/reference in the future, as you write more scripts. KMP Entertainment offers a wide range of screenwriting course and author services. Please check our website at www.kmpentertainment.org if you are interested in training beyond this challenge.

Again, congratulations on taking the first step in becoming a professional screenwriter! Now go get started!

Michelle Murray,
COO, KMP ENTERTAINMENT

THINGS YOU NEED BEFORE YOU START THE CHALLENGE

1 *A computer*

2 *Wifi/Internet service*

3 *Adequate time to devote to this endeavor*

4 *Desire to write a feature length screenplay*

5 *A story idea*

**Note

There are notes pages that follow the challenge activity pages. Each day, take notes in this section, as well as record your biggest takeaways. This will help you be more organized and efficient. It is also a great way to reference information in the future, after the challenge has been completed.

50 DAY

SCREENPLAY CHALLENGE

DAY 1

Research the concept "Show not Tell"

DAY 2

Practice! Write 6 sentences to show not tell what fear looks like for your character.

DAY 3

Practice! Write 6 sentences to show not tell what anger looks like for your character.

DAY 4

Practice! Write 6 sentences to show not tell what heartbreak looks like for your character.

DAY 5

Practice! Write 6 sentences to show not tell what happiness looks like for your character.

DAY 6

Practice! Write 6 sentences to show not tell what disgust looks like for your character.

DAY 7

Read this article: https://jerryjenkins.com/show-dont-tell/

DAY 8

Research "Premise in screenwriting."

DAY 9

Download and read this document: http://www.twoadverbs.com/logline.pdf

50 DAY

SCREENPLAY CHALLENGE

DAY 10

Read this article: https://scriptmag.com/features/7-crucial-logline-mistakes-fix

DAY 11

Search "John Truby Anatomy of Story" on youtube and watch entire interview.

DAY 12

Research The Writer's Guild of America

DAY 13

Write a FLASH FICTION of the story your script will be based on. 500 words or less.

DAY 14

Install Grammarly on your computer

DAY 15

Watch this video: https://www.youtube.com/watch?v=33FEuoNr6Zs

DAY 16

Research these terms: protagonist, antagonist and reflection character

DAY 17

Take this personality test as both your antagonist and protagonist: https://www.16personalities.com/free-personality-test

DAY 18

Use this formula to craft your logline for your screenplay: _____must_____ in order to _____

50 DAY

SCREENPLAY CHALLENGE

DAY 19

Research "evoking emotion in your writing"

DAY 20

Google "writing for emotional impact by Karl Iglesias pdf" Download the pdf from the lightleaks site and read it.

DAY 21

Purchase a copy of the Emotion Thesaurus

DAY 22

Google "how to write character descriptions in a screenplay"

DAY 23

Give thought to the following: What are the backstories of your protagonist and antagonist? What was their childhood like? Fave clothes? Occupation? Fave foods? Fave movie? What do they look like? etc

DAY 24

Research Hero's Journey

DAY 25

Research Archplot Structure. Download a pdf copy. You will use this structure to write your screenplay.

DAY 26

Watch the Matrix and look for the points of Archplot structure/Hero's Journey.

DAY 27

Watch The Princess and The Frog. Identify the points of Archplot Structure/the Hero's Journey.

50 DAY

SCREENPLAY CHALLENGE

DAY 28

Research "Vogler archetypes"

DAY 29

Research "What is a beat sheet in film?" Then write one for your screenplay. Do an outline, following the beats of Archplot structure, as well.

DAY 30

Research "how to write a scene in a script"

DAY 31

The industry software standard is Final Draft. Google and download a trial copy. Explore the software program and its features.

DAY 32

Research "7 deadly dialogue sins"

DAY 33

Search youtube for "Robert Mckee why is quality writing so rare?"

DAY 34

Search youtube for "How to make the audience care about your characters by John Truby."

DAY 35

You will write Act One of your screenplay. (Approximately 30 pgs of the total 120 pgs.) Page #s are listed at the bottom of your Archplot structure diagram to help you stay on track. Use Final Draft. Follow Archplot Structure. Today, write the Ordinary World scenes.

DAY 36

Write the scenes for the Call to Adventure.

50 DAY
SCREENPLAY CHALLENGE

DAY 37

Write the scenes for the Refusal of the Call.

DAY 38

Write the scenes for the Crossing The Threshold.

DAY 39

Act 1 is complete. Proofread/edit it. Expand your characters if needed and use the most evocative language possible.

DAY 40

Begin Act 2. Introduce tests, allies and enemies.

DAY 41

You're now at your screenplay's midpoint. Heighten the action.

DAY 42

Write the Approaching the Inmost Cave scenes.

DAY 43

End Act Two by writing your Inmost Cave scenes

DAY 44

Act 2 is done! Now proofread and revise it. Can you expand your characters to make them more appealing or more easily disliked by the audience? Can you heighten the action or make the story more cinematic with heightened stakes? If you can, do so.

DAY 45

Begin work on Act 3. Write your scenes for the Final Push. Things should be tense and the action high.

50 DAY

SCREENPLAY CHALLENGE

DAY 46

Write the scenes for Seizing the Sword. This is your story's climax. Make the audience unable to turn away.

DAY 47

Write your Return to the Elixir scenes. This is the aftermath of the Hero's Journey. What is life like after this journey?

DAY 48

Act 3 is done! Today, proofread and revise it as needed.

DAY 49

Read your script in its entirety. Is it cinematic? Does it use the most evocative language possible? Does it follow proper archplot structure? Do you have scenes that should be omitted because they don't move the story along? Revise, edit and proofread.

DAY 50

Congratulations! You have the first draft of a screenplay! Continue the revision process if needed.

Believe in yourself and your dreams. You belong in the room!

~Michelle Murray

DAY ONE

Notes

Biggest takeaways

DAY TWO

Notes

Biggest Takeaways

DAY THREE

Notes

Biggest Takeaways

DAY FOUR

Notes

Biggest takeaways

DAY FIVE

Notes.

Biggest Takeaways

DAY SIX

Notes

Biggest Takeaways

DAY SEVEN

Notes

Biggest Takeaways

DAY EIGHT

Notes

Biggest Takeaways

DAY NINE

Notes

Biggest Takeaways

DAY TEN

Notes

Biggest Takeaways

*Love yourself enough to discipline yourself.
Great job hanging in there for ten days! Now
keep pushing to the finish line.
Michelle*

DAY ELEVEN

Notes

Biggest Takeaways

DAY TWELVE

Notes

Biggest Takeaways

DAY THIRTEEN

Notes

Biggest Takeaways

DAY FOURTEEN

Notes

Biggest Takeaways

DAY FIFTEEN

Notes

Biggest Takeaways

DAY SIXTEEN

Notes

Biggest Takeaways

DAY SEVENTEEN

Notes

Biggest Takeaways

DAY EIGHTEEN

Notes

Biggest Takeaways

DAY NINETEEN

Notes

Biggest Takeaways

DAY TWENTY

Notes

Biggest Takeaways

You have a duty to yourself to never quit, and always have the work ethic to achieve your goals. You've got this! You belong in the room!
~Michelle Murray

DAY TWENTY-ONE

Notes

Biggest Takeaways

DAY TWENTY-TWO

Notes

Biggest Takeaways

DAY TWENTY- THREE

Notes

Biggest Takeaways

DAY TWENTY- FOUR

Notes

Biggest Takeaways

DAY TWENTY- FIVE

Notes

Biggest Takeaways

DAY TWENTY- SIX

Notes

Biggest Takeaways

DAY TWENTY- SEVEN

Notes

Biggest Takeaways

DAY TWENTY- EIGHT

Notes

Biggest Takeaways

DAY TWENTY- NINE

Notes

Biggest Takeaways

DAY THIRTY

Notes

Biggest Takeaways

DAY THIRTY ONE

Notes

Biggest Takeaways

DAY THIRTY TWO

Notes

Biggest Takeaways

Notes

Biggest Takeaways

DAY THIRTY FOUR

Notes

Biggest Takeaways

DAY THIRTY FIVE

Notes

Biggest Takeaways

DAY THIRTY SIX

Notes

Biggest Takeaways

DAY THIRTY SEVEN

Notes

Biggest Takeaways

DAY THIRTY EIGHT

Notes

Biggest Takeaways

DAY THIRTY NINE

Notes

Biggest Takeaways

DAY FORTY

Notes

Biggest Takeaways

Notes

Biggest Takeaways

DAY FORTY TWO

Notes

Biggest Takeaways

Notes

Biggest Takeaways

DAY FORTY FOUR

Notes

Biggest Takeaways

DAY FORTY FIVE

Notes

Biggest Takeaways

DAY FORTY SIX

Notes

Biggest Takeaways

Notes

Biggest Takeaways

DAY FORTY EIGHT

Notes

Biggest Takeaways

Notes

Biggest Takeaways

DAY FIFTY

Notes

Biggest Takeaways

REFLECTIONS

Reflect on the process of getting your screenplay written. What areas do you need to revisit? What are your plans now that the screenplay is finished? Be specific so that you can make a plan and execute.

REFLECTIONS

REFLECTIONS

REFLECTIONS

REFLECTIONS

REFLECTIONS

REFLECTIONS

REFLECTIONS

Now what?

Like many writers, you may be wondering how to achieve your next steps and set of goals. You may wonder how to pitch your script for a sale or use it as a writing sample to gain work.

KMP Entertainment would be honored to help you on your journey if you need assistance. We offer both a Master Writer course and an Advanced Master Writer Course where we focus on things like Intellectual Property law and contract law, as well as the pitch process, so that you understand how to negotiate a deal and how to monetize your creativity. We also offer consultation services and a number of other services to help complete and simplify the screenwriting process.

We'd love to work with you virtually or in person.

May you find much success on this creative path! Remember: you belong in the room!

www.kmpentertainment.org
Visit the SHOP NOW section